HIGH-INTEREST STEAM
SOCIAL MEDIA

HIGH-INTEREST STEAM

AUTOMOBILES

COSMETICS

DRONES

ENVIRONMENT

FASHION

GAMING

MUSIC

SMARTPHONES

SOCIAL MEDIA

SPORTS

HIGH-INTEREST STEAM

SOCIAL MEDIA

MARY DEAN

MASON CREST
PHILADELPHIA | MIAMI

MASON CREST
PO Box 221876
Hollywood, FL 33022
(866) MCP-BOOK (toll-free) • www.masoncrest.com

First printing

9 8 7 6 5 4 3 2 1
ISBN (hardback) 978-1-4222-4525-5
ISBN (series) 978-1-4222-4516-3
ISBN (ebook) 978-1-4222-7294-7

Library of Congress Cataloging-in-Publication Data

Names: Dean, Mary (Writer of children's books), author.
Title: Social media / Mary Dean.
Description: Hollywood, FL : Mason Crest, [2022] I
Series: High-interest STEAM I Includes bibliographical references and index.
Identifiers: LCCN 2020012994 I ISBN 9781422245255 (hardback) I
ISBN 9781422272947 (ebook)
Subjects: LCSH: Social media–Juvenile literature. I
Science–Juvenile literature.
Classification: LCC HM742 .D464 2022 I DDC 302.23/1–dc23
LC record available at https://lccn.loc.gov/2020012994

Developed and Produced by National Highlights, Inc.
Editor: Andrew Luke
Production: Crafted Content, LLC

QR CODES AND LINKS TO THIRD-PARTY CONTENT

CONTENTS

KEY ICONS TO LOOK FOR

Words to Understand: These words with their easy-to-understand definitions will increase the readers' understanding of the text while building vocabulary skills.

Sidebars: This boxed material within the main text allows readers to build knowledge, gain insights, explore possibilities, and broaden their perspectives by weaving together additional information to provide realistic and holistic perspectives.

Educational Videos: Readers can view videos by scanning our QR codes, providing them with additional educational content to supplement the text. Examples include news coverage, moments in history, speeches, iconic sports moments, and much more!

Text-Dependent Questions: These questions send the reader back to the text for more careful attention to the evidence presented there.

Research Projects: Readers are pointed toward areas of further inquiry connected to each chapter. Suggestions are provided for projects that encourage deeper research and analysis.

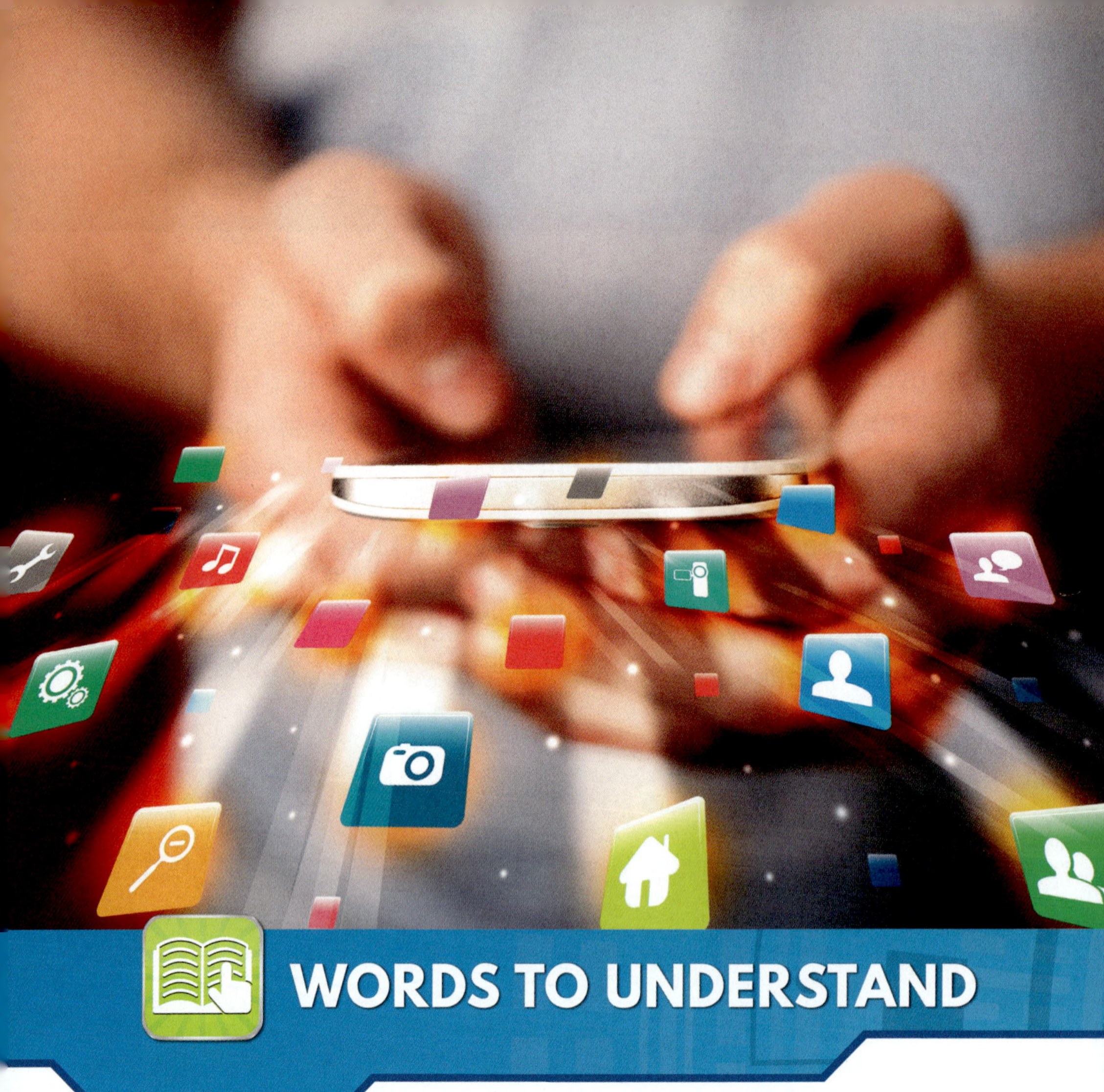

WORDS TO UNDERSTAND

circadian rhythm—a natural biological process that regulates the sleep and wake cycle

cited—to be quoted in another work for the purpose of validating or providing evidence regarding a statement or idea

dopamine—a compound present in the body as a neurotransmitter and a precursor of other substances including epinephrine

CHAPTER 1

SCIENCE IN SOCIAL MEDIA

Did you know that 2.65 billion people worldwide use social media today? This means that almost everyone you know probably has at least one social media account. Social media helps people to connect with friends and family members, meet new people, buy products, and even advertise various businesses and products. Social media users employ "likes" and "shares" to communicate their approval of certain ideas and images, which is where it gets interesting. We can look to science to explain why social media is so enticing, and how businesses use these platforms to engage new customers.

PSYCHOLOGY AND SOCIAL MEDIA

Psychology is a branch of science that deals with the way we think and how we do things in our day-to-day lives. Even though this branch doesn't deal with beakers or test tubes, it is still a demonstrably valid branch of science since it follows all the same basic rules as the other branches of science. For example, psychologists and therapists use hypotheses and conduct social experiments to prove certain theories and to change the world, one person at a time.

When you think about social media, one of the biggest things that may come to mind is "likes." Platforms like Facebook, Instagram, and Twitter all use a "like" system for users to communicate their feelings about certain thoughts, ideas, and images that come across in their social media accounts. Tapping the heart or the thumbs-up symbol that accompanies every post communicates your approval of the post to the person who posted it. Facebook takes this a step further by allowing additional "reactions," allowing users to indicate sadness, anger, or laughter at posts. In today's society, getting a large number of likes is highly coveted, which has roots in psychology.

Psychology and "Likes" on Social Media

A big part of why social media has become what it is today is due to the way it makes us feel. Studies have shown that the reaction that happens in our brains when we get likes and comments on social media is similar to the reaction that occurs when we eat chocolate or hug a loved one. Psychology tells us that the reason we feel warm and fuzzy inside at these times is due to the release of **dopamine**, otherwise known as "the happy chemical," in our brains.

To understand why we love things (such as social media) that cause our brains to release dopamine as much as we do, we must first understand how the brain processes the world around us. Think of the human brain as a group of circuits. Each of these circuits serves a specific purpose. Some of them are responsible for helping us to avoid danger, reminding us to eat and drink, and telling

Validation from the reactions of others to items users share is a big part of why people enjoy social media.

us when it's time to go to sleep. The portion of the brain that is activated when we surf social media is called the "reward center."

The circuits in the reward center of our brain communicate with one another using dopamine. In other words, when something good happens to us, such as getting a like on social media, dopamine levels in our brains increase, which is what elicits those happy emotions that you might have experienced when interacting on social media. When something undesirable happens, like someone posting a negative comment on one of your posts, dopamine levels decrease, which has the opposite effect.

Another chemical that makes social media so enticing is oxytocin. Also known as "the cuddle chemical," oxytocin is often released when we kiss or hug a loved one. How does this relate to social media? Recent studies show that when we interact online via social media, oxytocin levels can rise up to 13 percent. With that spike in levels, we experience feelings of love and trust and also feel less stressed.

OXYTOCIN AND RELATIONSHIPS ONLINE

One research study set out to see just how much people feel others can be trusted online. This study asked participants from several different social media sites how trustworthy they thought people were online. Facebook users showed the highest numbers, with 43 percent of users agreeing that others can be trusted. This is likely related to the release of oxytocin in the brain while on social media, since this hormone elicits feelings of love and trust.

The danger that the rewards system poses, especially when it comes to social media, is addiction. When your brain starts to rely on things such as likes, comments, and shares to activate the dopamine and oxytocin surges in your brain, you might find yourself obsessively checking your notifications or getting irritable when you don't have access to your social accounts. These are both examples of side effects of social media addiction, and when you experience them, it is a strong sign that you should cut back your usage.

So-called social media addiction is another hot-button topic when it comes to psychology. When most people think about addiction, cigarettes and illegal drugs might come to mind. Many people don't realize that excessively obsessing about or using social media can also constitute addiction. While it is not an official behavioral disorder yet, the *Diagnostic and Statistical Manual of Mental Disorders* (*DSM*) lists social media addiction as a "condition for further study." Psychologists are working to find new ways to

Social media addiction is not an official mental disorder, but the American Psychiatric Society is studying it.

curb social media obsession by limiting the amount of time patients spend online and having them take frequent breaks when engaging in social media interactions.

SOCIAL MEDIA MARKETING AND PSYCHOLOGY

A big part of the community that uses social media includes network marketers. These entrepreneurs use platforms like Facebook and Instagram to reach their audience to sell items or distribute information about them. Social media marketing has proven to be a very lucrative business; in 2020, ad spending was forecasted to hit $102,292 million. This number is expected to grow by seven percent by 2023.

Targeted Advertising and Psychology

Psychology plays a major part in the success of social media marketing in a few major ways. In order to be successful, online marketers have to understand their target audience and how to engage with them. Psychology explains a phenomenon called **circadian rhythm** that helps marketers place ads strategically in order to make the most money or engage the largest audience possible.

Circadian rhythm tells marketers that social media subscribers are most likely to engage in high-arousal posts—posts that are intended to make us feel stress, fear, or anger—in the morning. These are the types of posts that are created to engage an audience and start a conversation. Sometimes, these are intended to sell a product but can also be used to sell an idea such as the need to purchase life insurance.

During lunch time or mid-afternoon, research shows that people's brains are more apt to engage in posts that require us to think. These posts might distribute scientific information, or they could include "boosted" posts, which are posts that marketers pay a fee to distribute to their audience. Understanding the psychology of when people are most receptive to certain types of information makes a huge difference in the profitability of social media marketing.

THE PSYCHOLOGY OF MEMES

Most people who surf social media sites have seen a meme from time to time. A meme is a photo, gif, or video that is spread around on social media to convey an idea. Most of the time, these are

Memes are created to elicit a variety of reactions, from happiness and laughter to fear and anger.

created to be humorous, but some memes also trigger different emotions such as anger, fear, and hate. Although the science of memes is hard to study because it is laden with intangible elements, psychologists have taken a stab at trying to define what makes them so popular.

When a meme gains considerable popularity on social media, it is classified as viral. Research shows that it doesn't matter how high-quality or how true a meme's basis is—it can still be popular. What is more important is how emotionally arousing the meme itself is. In other words, if a meme makes you feel something, it has a much better chance of becoming viral.

This video explains the science behind why memes and other things on social media go viral.

SOCIAL MEDIA AND THE SCIENCE COMMUNITY

Social media has proven to be useful for more than just connecting with old friends and sharing viral memes. The science community has used social media to catapult its ideas, research, and studies to the community and the world. Using platforms such as Facebook and Twitter, the way scientists collaborate, distribute, and cite research studies has changed dramatically.

Science and Twitter

Twitter is most well known for its short posts of 280 characters or fewer. Celebrities, internet influencers, and even the president of the United States use Twitter to share their thoughts and emotions. Even though these interactions are usually social in nature, the social media platform has gained traction among the science community as well. Nowadays, scientists use Twitter to find information on studies similar to their own, to collaborate with other scientists, and to distribute scientific findings and other information to the world.

To communicate scientific findings, to collaborate on projects, and to find research studies and articles to cite in their own work, scientists have discovered the power of the tweet. Research shows that frequently shared articles on Twitter are much more likely to be **cited** in other works. This means that if a scientist in any field wants to gain traction online, using Twitter is a great way to help them get there.

Twitter allows users to share thoughts, opinions, information and reactions to the entire planet instantly.

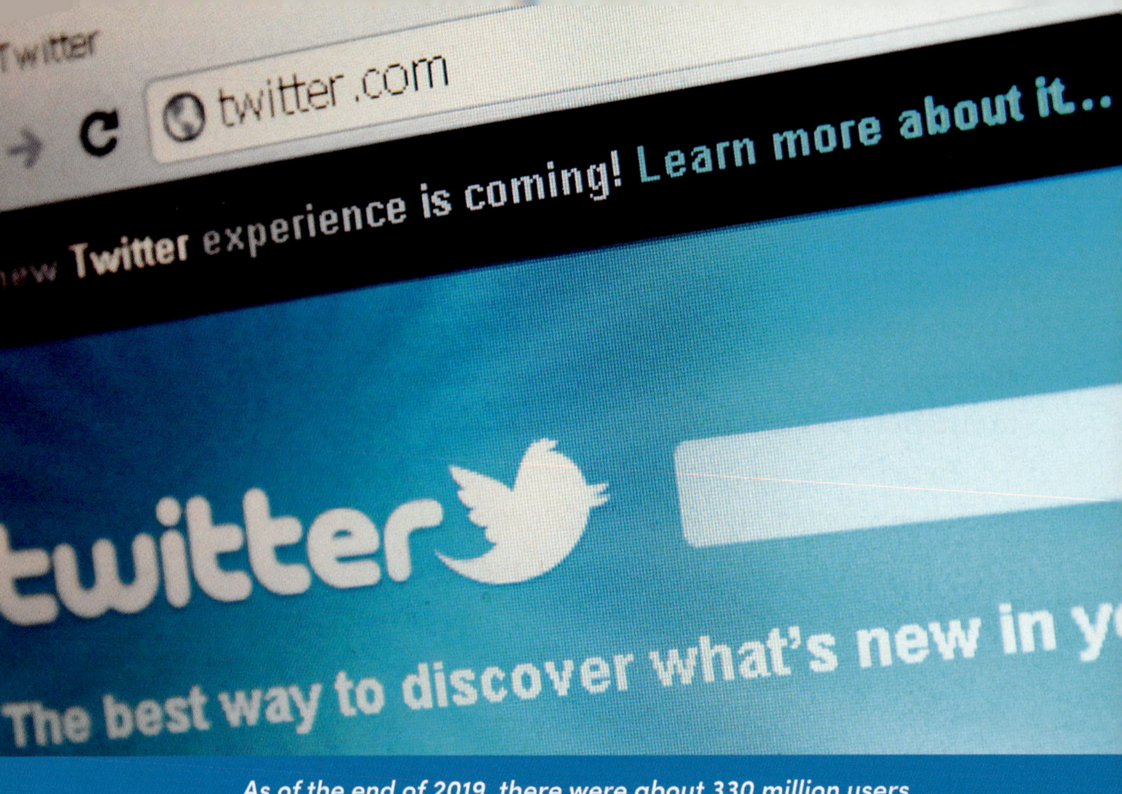

As of the end of 2019, there were about 330 million users on the Twitter platform.

Twitter can also help scientists distribute their information to people outside their industry or community. By publishing and sharing their research and scientific conclusions on Twitter, scientists reach the general public easier than ever before. This widens a scientist's network and outreach, which is important, since paying attention to science can tell us more about the world around us, including how and why it works.

Science and Facebook

The group feature on Facebook helps unite those who are interested in or participate in science-related subjects. Very few of these groups on Facebook talk about all branches of science. Instead, they focus on one or two. For instance, groups might specialize in astronomy and physics or food and nutrition. These groups might be comprised of science enthusiasts or people who are actively engaged in working in the science field.

Regardless of the career or stature of the members of the group, Facebook has opened a larger conversation about science to the world around us. By connecting people with similar scientific interests, a network of brains is created—which can help further expand scientific research and can also help perfect hypotheses, Both are important to the field of science since asking questions and forming ideas is at the root of science as a whole.

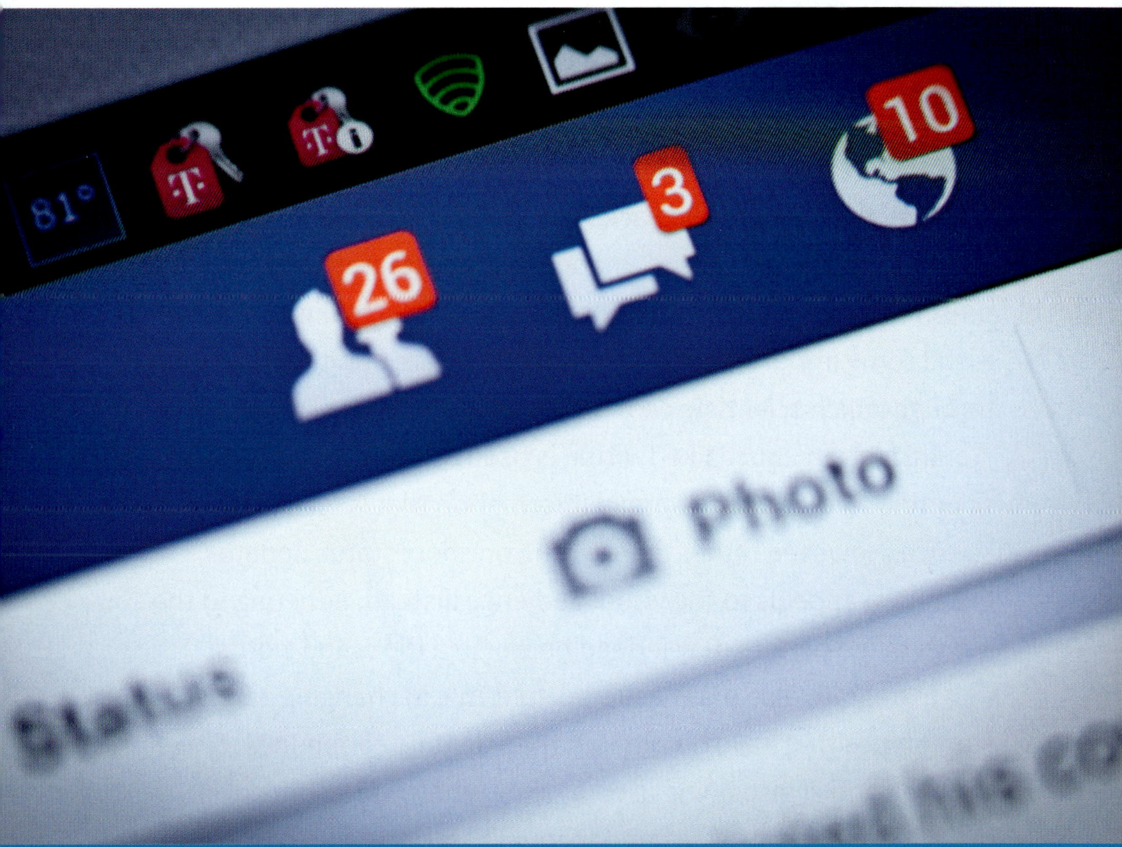

Notifications on Facebook indicate the number of friend requests, instant messages and other features.

NEWS YOU CAN USE

Across the Facebook science communities, the most predominant posts tout science "news you can use." These posts might feature information about what foods to eat for the best health benefits or when to go outside and see astronomical events such as meteor showers or eclipses. One study across 30 science-related pages showed that these types of posts made up 20 percent of page content.

Science and Other Social Media Platforms

In addition to Twitter and Facebook, science also has a presence on other big platforms such as Snapchat and Instagram. Although this presence is less prevalent on these social media mainstays, there is still some importance to them since they are additional channels through which scientists can further their outreach.

Instagram, much like Twitter, is used as a platform to share scientific studies and to spread information that is learned through science. However, rather than relying on short status updates, Instagram appeals to the visual audience instead, adhering to the adage that a picture may indeed be worth a thousand words.

Instagram also plays an important role in changing gender stereotypes that have dominated the scientific community. Since this platform is also being used to show photos of scientists in real situations, improved gender equality is becoming more and more apparent. More specifically, better representation of female

Instagram is a primarily visual platform for sharing user images.

scientists could change the way scientific findings are perceived. A 2018 Qualtrics survey showed that not only did images of female scientists on Instagram lead to perceptions that science is less exclusively male, but also led to participants perceiving "scientists as significantly warmer than did participants who saw science-only images or control images."

Snapchat, being one of the most prevalent social platforms known today, is also crucial to sharing scientific information. Even though Snapchat mainly focuses on erasable messages, newer updates have made it possible to share scientific articles. There are also specialized Snapchat accounts that are dedicated to discussing and spreading information about all fields of science.

The Snapchat platform relies heavily on the augmented reality (AR) experience it can offer users.

TEXT-DEPENDENT QUESTIONS

1. What is the difference between dopamine and oxytocin?
2. What is one factor that can help a meme go viral?
3. What is one way that Twitter enhances access to scientific information?

RESEARCH PROJECT

Social media is more than just a platform we use to communicate with one another and plan big events. When it comes to science, Facebook, Instagram, Snapchat, and Twitter, all play a role. Imagine that you have been assigned the duty of creating a new social media platform that is dedicated to serving the scientific community. First, research the different ways that social media and science interact with one another. Then, create a presentation that details what features your platform would include for both scientists and science enthusiasts. What impact might your platform make on the science community today? What long-term impacts might your platform have on science and the world? Complete your presentation visually either on a poster board or via digital slideshow.

WORDS TO UNDERSTAND

algorithm—a procedure for solving a mathematical problem in a finite number of steps that frequently involves repetition of an operation

augmented reality—an enhanced version of reality created by the use of technology to overlay digital information on an image of something being viewed through a device

metadata—a combination of virtual data that gives information about other data

microprocessor—a component of a computer that processes data contained on an integrated circuit chip within a smartphone

CHAPTER 2

TECHNOLOGY IN SOCIAL MEDIA

The prevalence of social media in today's society has a lot to do with the technology that supports it. Frequently used features such as built-in photo editors and two-way video chats are a couple of examples of technology-driven capabilities. Beneath the surface, information storage and enhanced privacy on social media can also be attributed to technology.

THE TECHNOLOGY BEHIND SHARING PHOTOS

Sharing photos dominates a huge portion of social media across all the major platforms like Snapchat, Facebook, Instagram, and Twitter. Photos have become such a large part of what we share that 1.8 billion photos are posted to social media daily. These numbers mean that in less than a week, there is a photo uploaded for every person alive on the planet, including those in undeveloped countries that have no internet access at all.

3D Photos

In May 2018, Facebook launched its revolutionary 3D photo technology. This technology allows viewers to see photos with more depth of field and from a variety of perspectives. The basis is simple: as you tilt and rotate your device, the photo on the screen tilts and rotates as well. The subject matter in the photo itself also appears more realistic and life-like, which enhances users' browsing experience. So how does this feature work?

The process starts in the **microprocessor** of the mobile device that captures the image. Previously, creating a 3D image required multiple pictures to be taken and then combined. However, modern technology has made the process easier and simpler for social media users. Now, when a phone's camera is used, the technology within it automatically creates a depth map.

When a multi-camera smartphone is used to capture an image, it automatically generates a depth map, which is necessary to produce a 3D image.

The next step involves a special **algorithm**. This algorithm uses the depth map and combines it with small movements that are captured by the phone's motion detection systems. Once these two are combined, a smooth, well-rounded depth map is generated. If the process is stopped here, however, the subject in the foreground would still appear flat to the viewer.

The final step in creating these photos is perhaps the most interesting part of the process. This part of the process involves the technology "imagining" what the rest of the photo might look like. It makes "assumptions" that are used to fill in any gaps in the image. If there is hair on the top of a head, this hair will likely continue through the image. The person's skin tone can also be continued accordingly. In addition, other textures and shapes are estimated to create the stunning multi-perspective images that we see today.

GIF Images

GIFs, or Graphics Interchange Format images, are a prevalent way that people convey thoughts and emotions on social media. These looped images are utilized by a staggering amount of users, with more than 330 million people searching for GIFs monthly. Even though GIFs have been around since the birth of the internet, they have gained traction through the widespread availability of high-speed internet and the increase in meme culture.

GIF images are popular among social media users, especially the younger crowd, for a few reasons. First, they are a quick and quirky way for users to express themselves online. Second, they help people convey their thoughts in a deeply personal way since the pop culture typically associated with each GIF is telling of their personality and interests. Finally, they are a large part of meme culture, which has been boosted by social media in recent years.

A GIF is a quickly changing combination of multiple photo frames that works similar to how an animated flipbook does.

Anyone who uses GIFs on his or her social media platforms can thank technology for them. When it comes to technology, GIFs are relatively simple to construct, take up a small amount of space, and use lossless compression, which allows them to animate images without sacrificing picture quality.

GIFs are digital files that move like a short loop of a video. However, the image file itself is not a moving format. Actually, these images are a combination of multiple photo frames that quickly change. This gives the image the illusion of moving, much like an animated flipbook would. This method of combining the images makes for a piece of imagery that is quickly uploaded and accessible on almost any platform that has access to the internet.

GIF OR JIFF?

Across social media, there is a widespread debate about how to pronounce the acronym for Graphics Interchange Format. Although Steve Wilhite, who created the original GIF, says it is pronounced "jiff," many people still refer to the image by pronouncing it with a hard "g."

Photo Filters

Instagram and Snapchat are two of the largest social media platforms that depend mostly on sharing images in today's society. One of the most popular features that these platforms offer is the capability of applying filters to your images. Instagram focuses on adding filters that perfect users' skin tone and other aesthetic elements. Snapchat has some of the same features but takes it a step further by offering **augmented reality** models that add virtual makeup, animal ears, and more to users' images.

Instagram filters work by tuning colors and textures in images according to a specific set of rules set by technology programmers. Each of the filters that are preloaded into Instagram's platform manipulates images the same way. However, they can come out looking different, since the way their presets interact with each image depends on how warm or cool the original image is, how much lighting is present, and much more. For example, the "Clarendon" filter on Instagram works by intensifying shadows and brightening highlights in your images.

The selfie is such a popular social media phenomenon that platforms build technology specifically to work with them.

Snapchat filters take on more complicated technology by utilizing face detection, facial landmark recognition, and image processing to produce the user designed result. This combination of processes makes it possible for users to create images of themselves with flower crowns, glasses, and even images of their faces on different bodies. Here is a breakdown of each step in the process to get there:

- To begin, Snapchat uses face detection software, which divides the image into virtual triangles. Then, a sliding window is used to determine whether a certain shape is a face or not. In simpler terms, Snapchat's technology will slide a virtual window around different shapes until it finds a face within the image.
- The next step in the process involves facial landmark recognition software. This is different from facial detection because it aims

to locate features on the face, such as the eyes, nose, and mouth. This technology works by taking the portion of the photo that facial detection has identified and breaking it into smaller sections. First, facial landmark software creates a virtual field around the face of a subject. Then, it uses built-in mathematical programs to determine where facial features are most likely to be in relation to this silhouette.

- The final step is image processing. Now that the technology has determined where the face in the image is and where the main points of the face are, digital images are placed on top. This is where the bunny ears or virtual accessories are processed on top of an image.

Platforms such as Snapchat use facial detection technology.

TECHNOLOGY AND COMMUNICATING ON SOCIAL MEDIA

People have been able to pick up a mobile phone and talk to one another for many years, but recently, the prevalence of two-way video chat has become more prominent. With as many as one in five people on social media using video chat capabilities daily, this makes up for an essential part of social media in today's world.

The technology responsible for making two-way video chat possible involves several different steps. The first is signaling. This process is relatively simple—it just involves setting up a connection between two people. Primary information, such as key data, **metadata**, and messages, first need to be communicated. This establishes a primary connection between two people who want to connect via video and audio.

Next, the two people need to connect to one another virtually. In order to understand how two people connect over the internet, you must first understand how the internet gives each person an identity. The "identity" of a person on the internet is called an IP address. This combination of letters and numbers is a unique identifier and includes personal information such as a user's geolocation. Once both IP addresses are identified and verified over the platform's database, a connection is then established.

Once two people's IP addresses are connected, it is then time for the platform to relay the media. Each social media website has its own server that is dedicated to completing actions like these. The technology within these servers allows for the photo and video information, which is processed through the phone, tablet, or computer, to be transferred via the internet, and displayed to the person to whom the message was sent.

This video explains how a video chat platform is built from the ground up.

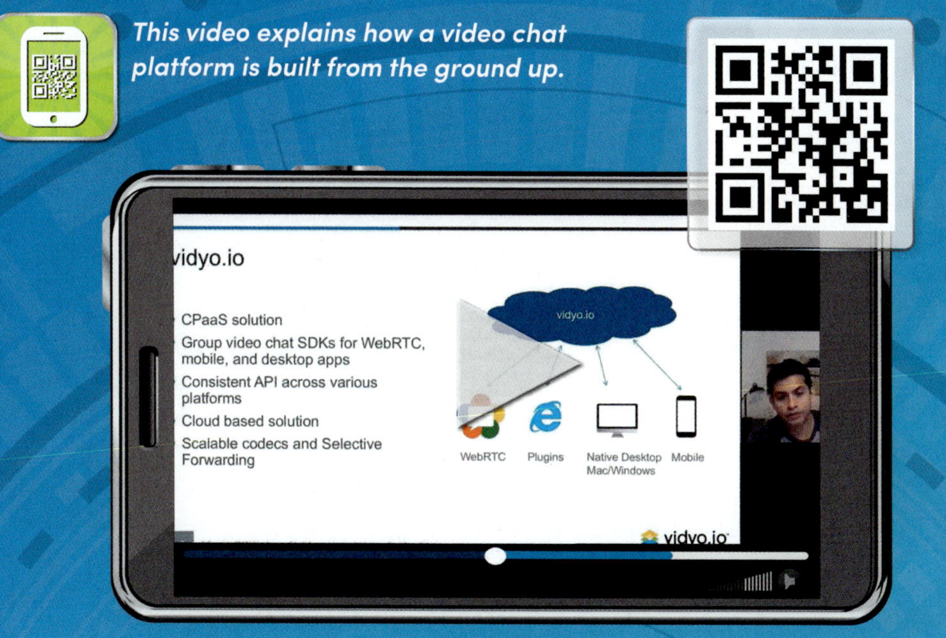

DEVICES AND SOCIAL MEDIA

Phones and tablets are the number one most crucial part of making social media what it has become today. Without the addition of the mobile element, social media would not be the same. In the early days, computers were the best way to connect to others on these platforms. In modern society, though, smartphones and tablets have prevailed, making social media the formidable, omnipresent thing that it is nowadays.

While all three of these devices are used to access social media today, mobile devices like smartphones are certainly the most commonly used. More than ¾ of the audiences of Facebook and Instagram primarily use their smartphones to access their social media accounts. This is largely due to how convenient it is to use mobile devices to share tidbits of our lives on social media.

Mobile technology has made social media available from almost anywhere, and social media platforms have all adapted their technology accordingly.

It seems like everyone in today's society is always on the go. Now, you can take your social profiles with you to the coffee shop or the grocery store, meaning it's more accessible than it has ever been, and it's all thanks to technology.

Smartphone applications are specifically designed to make social platforms like Facebook and Instagram more mobile-friendly. In fact, these applications are so popular, that in 2018, Facebook's mobile application was downloaded an estimated 711 million times. Instagram was downloaded about 444 million times as well. This means that the technology that allows us to manufacture apps such as these is crucial to the growth and longevity of social media as a whole.

CYBER SECURITY ON SOCIAL MEDIA

The popularity of social media has brought about a major conversation concerning the importance of cyber security. As social media users,

CYBER SECURITY FAIL!

Unfortunately, the focus on cyber security in regard to social media today was partly brought on by failures in the system. Data security breaches on Facebook in 2018 sparked a heated lawsuit and a push for more security on social media networks as a whole.

there are several things we do to protect our private information, such as using unique usernames and complex passwords to protect our accounts. In addition to this, creators of social media platforms also developed more complex cyber security measures that help to further protect the information we share and otherwise talk about online.

One version of this security is called end-to-end encryption and mostly has to do with private messaging across social media platforms. This form of cyber security aims to make it impossible for hackers or other internet-savvy criminals to access the conversations in your inbox.

Basically, when you begin a conversation on a messaging app such as Facebook Messenger, two "keys" are created—one for you and one for the person you are messaging. When you send a message to this person, your words are translated into an indiscernible code that is transmitted over the internet. Once it reaches the person it is meant for, the special key that was created is then used to translate the message back into a language that you can understand. This prevents anyone from intercepting the message between point A and point B, which would violate your privacy.

Arguably the most fascinating thing about this process is its automation. Even the creator of the process wouldn't likely be able to unlock your information before it reaches its desired person. This is because the technology built into the end-to-end encryption randomizes the process used to protect your message, so it's almost impossible to determine how a key will be created. As a result, you can rest easy knowing your information is protected.

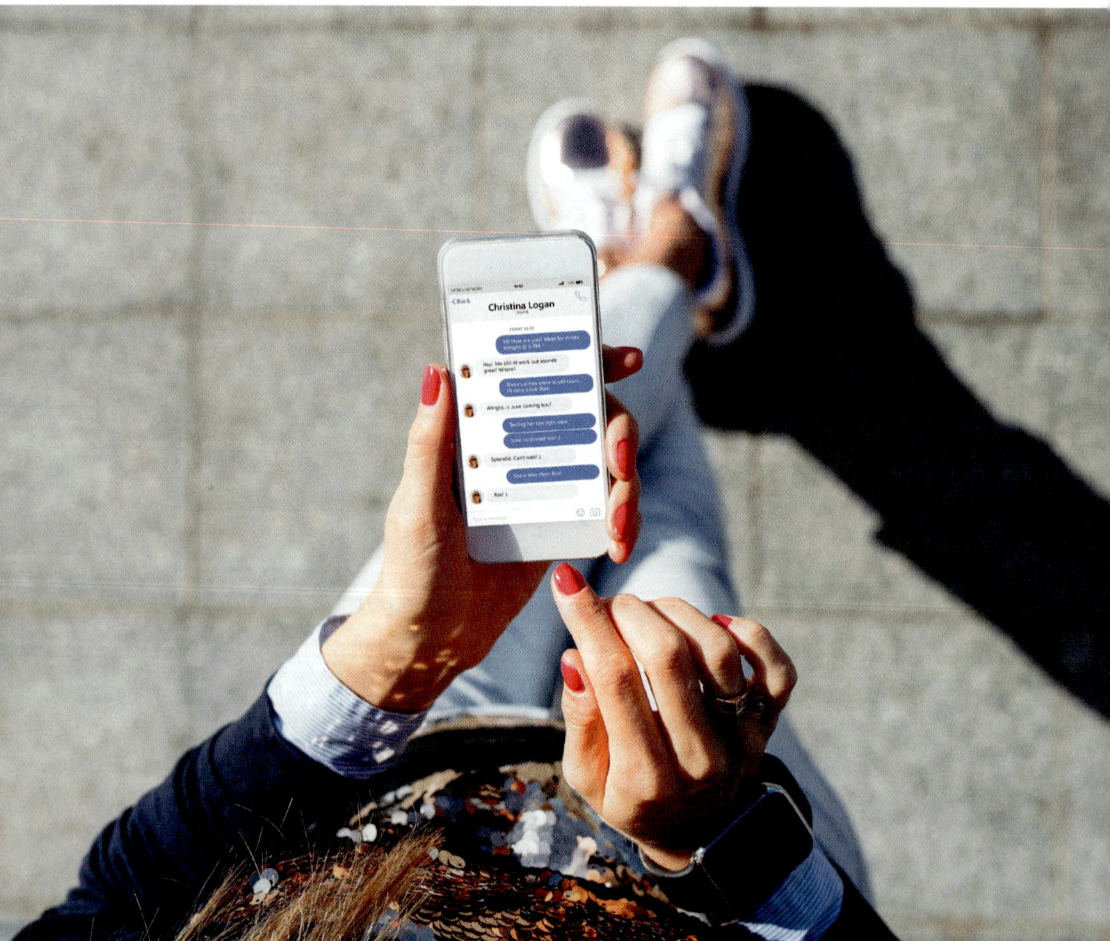

Digital conversations are encrypted when sent to deter criminals from intercepting them.

TEXT-DEPENDENT QUESTIONS

1. When did Facebook release its 3D photo technology?
2. What is one reason why GIF images are so popular among social media users?
3. What makes instant messaging secure?

RESEARCH PROJECT

Technology has played an enormous role in making social media what it is today. Research at least three technological advances that have enhanced the experience of social media users. Then, explain how each of these advances has changed the way we use social media today. Consider the following questions while you complete your research: How have each of these technological advances made a difference in the lives of social media users? How has each of these processes changed the way we think about social media today?

WORDS TO UNDERSTAND

data packet— a small file containing metadata that describes the structure and contents of the package, and resources such as data files that form the contents of the package

HTML—Hypertext Markup Language: a system which was created to build platforms on World Wide Web pages

server—a computer in a network that is used to access files or share peripherals, route e-mail, or otherwise communicate with other computers in the network

CHAPTER 3

ENGINEERING IN SOCIAL MEDIA

Engineering is a vital part of the puzzle that creates social media. Engineers work to build the platforms we use, store our information, enhance our experience, and fix our problems. No social media platform is perfect, but when a strong team of engineers is present, we can count on these platforms to keep growing and to become more and more relevant to our everyday lives. If you have ever used social media to play a game, access an application, or store data or information, you can champion engineers for allowing you to do so.

ENGINEERING ON SOCIAL MEDIA PLATFORMS

Software engineering is responsible in part for social media capabilities today. Engineering in social media platforms is one of the reasons why features such as marketing, storing profile information and messages, and many more are successful. Engineers that specialize in several different departments all work together to make social media the huge part of our lives that it is.

Software Engineering

Software engineers have made possible thousands of popular applications including games, messaging applications, tools for social media marketing, and social media platforms themselves.

Software Engineering and Video Games

Facebook games such as FarmVille have taken the world by storm. Since eight million people worldwide have played FarmVille 2 every day, it's safe to say that software engineers have made a sizeable impact on making Facebook not only functional but also fun. The process of building a game such as this has deep roots in software engineering.

Game developers build video games on Facebook using Unity, the most popular game engine in the world. A game engine is the architecture developers use to run the game. Facebook and Unity engineers integrated the two platforms to make it seamless for game developers building on Unity to export their finished games to Facebook.

Games and game engines are written in a specified code known as a programming language, the most popular of which is C++. For the web-based games preferred by many social media users, **HTML** (Hypertext Markup Language) is a powerful language. It is "a standardized system for tagging text files to achieve font, color, graphic, and hyperlink effects on web pages." With the implementation of HTML5 in 2014, the language evolved to be more interactive, with definitions for elements used for multimedia, graphics and interactivity. Although software engineers aren't

Games like FarmVille and dozens of others have achieved global success on Facebook.

responsible for creating the graphics that we see, they build the skeleton of the game. The code that they write tells the computer when to launch a game, how to save our progress as we play, and where to store our pertinent information like usernames and passwords within our profiles.

Software engineers are also responsible for making games on social media feel more lifelike. Storylines, game audio, lighting, sounds, and effects are just a few examples of things that need to be coded into video games. By understanding how to write in the language that computers and other technological devices can understand, software engineers can create larger-than-life, enticing games for you to play with your friends and family members.

WORKING TOGETHER THROUGH SOCIAL MEDIA

Engineers are using social media as a tool to collaborate and better organize their team agenda. Using social media networks such as Facebook and LinkedIn, engineers can build strong teams, organize workloads more effectively, and gain valuable insight into how to be more successful and productive when working on new projects.

Software Engineering and Messaging

Social media is now a significant tool that helps many people to keep in contact with their friends and family members. One of the most popular ways to do this is through messaging applications such as Facebook Messenger, Instagram DMs, and Snapchat's messaging feature. Software engineers not only create the programs that allow us to communicate with one another through these platforms, but they are also often responsible for maintaining the **servers** that store our information and keep it safe from cyber criminals.

Building the applications that we use to chat with our friends and family members is a crucial part of the job of any software engineer. These programs need to be reliable, fast, and easy to use for anyone that accesses them. Software engineers must anticipate the needs of people that use messaging platforms, integrate ways to make messaging quick and simple, and always be on the lookout for the next best thing.

Messaging apps are constantly evolving and improving to be as user-friendly as possible.

Today, one of the things that makes messaging on social media so enticing is our ability to see when someone is typing a message or has read one that we have sent. You may or may not be surprised to learn that software engineers are responsible for allowing us to see both of these things. When software engineers write the code for the messaging platforms we use, they must insert specific information in order to give us these capabilities.

Read receipts are one example of a commonly used feature that engineering has brought upon the world of social media. This real-time notification is triggered because the software within has been engineered to send a **data packet** to the platform's servers whenever a message is read. When you begin to reply, another packet is sent every few seconds as you type. When you send the message, the process restarts and manifests itself to the person you are communicating to on the other end.

KEEPING THE CONVERSATION ALIVE

Today, one of the reasons why people are so compelled to communicate through messaging platforms is due to their interactive nature. The capability to see when someone has read your message and when they are responding gives messaging a living, breathing aspect. This feature helps us to maintain a transparent conversation that is predictable and easy to understand for all parties.

Software Engineering and Social Media Marketing

Software engineering also focuses on creating programs that social media marketers use to push their products and ideas to the world. These programs are built in a way that optimizes when users see ads, who sees them, and for how long. Just as we discussed in the previous section, it is important to focus on these aspects of engagement in order to generate the most revenue or command the most attention of the target audience.

We know that software engineers write the code that forms the programs that we use to market to others on social media. In addition to building the skeleton of these programs, software engineers are also responsible for building a virtual clock into their code. Since circadian rhythm plays such an important role in social media marketing, it is imperative that the software engineer who creates marketing programs builds this into their code. The way this is done is similar to writing video game codes, except it uses the time of day

SOCIAL MEDIA MARKETING REVENUE

One of the major ways that platforms like Facebook generate revenue to operate and pay their employees is through ad sales. This market has been so successful that in 2018, their reported net income was $22.1 billion. If that wasn't impressive enough, their total revenue for the same year was reported at $55.8 billion. That makes for a net profit margin of 39.6 percent. Talk about some dough!

With the lure of its global reach and ability to target specific demographics, Facebook makes billions of dollars a year selling ads.

and special algorithms for target audiences to reach the people who are most likely to purchase products or subscribe to services.

Software Engineering and the Platforms

The most important part of social media is the platform itself. Everything you see from the text on the page, to the pictures, logos, links, and applications, are all created by software engineers. There are other people who take the engineering team's programs and enhance them, such as graphic designers and other professionals, but building the framework is almost entirely the job of software engineers.

Software engineers are charged with the job of creating an intuitive and engaging platform that is aesthetically pleasing and convenient to use. Every time you click an icon to navigate to your social media notifications or update your profile, you are completing actions via means that were designed by a software engineer.

Data Center Engineering

The role of a data center engineer is to create, maintain, and fix the physical servers where social media platforms live. These engineers build computers that process our information, create servers where it can be stored, troubleshoot these devices when they have errors, and in some cases, they are even responsible for maintaining the temperature and air quality in the buildings where these items are stored so that they can work at maximum capacity.

All of the information that we see on social media and all the programs that make it possible are housed in a building full of computers and other high-tech devices. These devices run 24 hours a day, 7 days a week, and are constantly accessing and storing

Data center engineers have to plan for every contingency to keep those facilities up and running smoothly around the clock.

millions of pieces of information every second. Since these devices have moving parts that are constantly in motion, overheating is a factor that must be safeguarded against. Data center engineers design technology such as cooling systems that prevent this type of malfunction from happening.

Another role of a data center engineer is fixing flaws within the data center. When a bug or other problem presents itself, the issue must be dealt with quickly and with the utmost attention and precision. One wrong move could cause the social platform to crash, or it could corrupt large amounts of data, which could negatively impact the experience of users across the platform. Since social media networks make most of their money from advertising, it is imperative that their users are confident that their information is safe and that they can depend on their social media platforms to constantly stay up and running.

Luckily, data center engineers are highly trained professionals who have the knowledge needed to fix problems quickly and accurately so that no one has to have a bad experience when they log in to their account. Some techniques that a data center engineer might use to fix a problem include inspecting cables for poor connections, remedying problems that cause their devices to overheat, and constantly looking for new ways to make processes simpler and faster.

Another huge part of this job is continuing to learn. The industry changes rapidly, so a continuously updated education is essential since technological advances periodically impact the way servers and computers are used in relation to all social media platforms.

Social Engineering

Social engineering is a malicious process that cyber criminals use to capture personal information from users on social media platforms. This information is used to steal identities, swindle money, and to do many other illegal things online. Some techniques that are used in

Cyber security has become a huge industry due in part to the spread of social media, and the amount of data available to be stolen from the major platforms.

Watch this in-depth description of who social engineers are, what they do, and how they do it.

this process are phishing, identity theft, and spam. This is not a new process or one that is specific to those using social media, but it has unfortunately become a commonplace action on these platforms because of the variety of people available to exploit.

One of the major ways that social engineers capture private information is through malicious emails. Users will receive an email that appears to come from Facebook or Instagram when being taken advantage of through a scam such as this. In some cases, these emails will contain links that lead users to enter their password or other sensitive information. Then, hackers capture this information to gain access to accounts.

With access, the personal information of the account user can be exploited, but it doesn't stop there. Now that the hacker has access to this person's account, the hacker can contact friends and family members of the victimized user and further exploit the situation. Since the messages will appear to be coming from someone that they know and trust, they are much more likely to divulge their sensitive information.

Social engineering is also used to create fake links to lure users into visiting malicious websites. These links might promise fake information about celebrity deaths or fraudulent schemes such as free computers or tablets. When an unsuspecting person clicks the link, malicious software could be downloaded onto their phone or computer that could steal private information by corrupting personal files and searching for other stored information.

Even though social engineering wasn't created with the purpose of helping social media operate, it is still a crucial part of what users should understand about the risks of social media. They should be aware of this type of engineering so that they can protect themselves and their personal information online.

Social engineering preys on our social media habits to enable cyber crimes such as phishing.

TEXT-DEPENDENT QUESTIONS

1. What are software engineers responsible for doing in regard to video games on social media?
2. What are two things that a data center engineer is expected to do?
3. Why is it important to understand what social engineering is and how it is executed?

RESEARCH PROJECT

Engineering has revolutionized social media as we know it today. Do some research to select and detail three aspects of engineering that you consider to be most crucial to how social media has developed. Put together a PowerPoint to present your findings to the class.

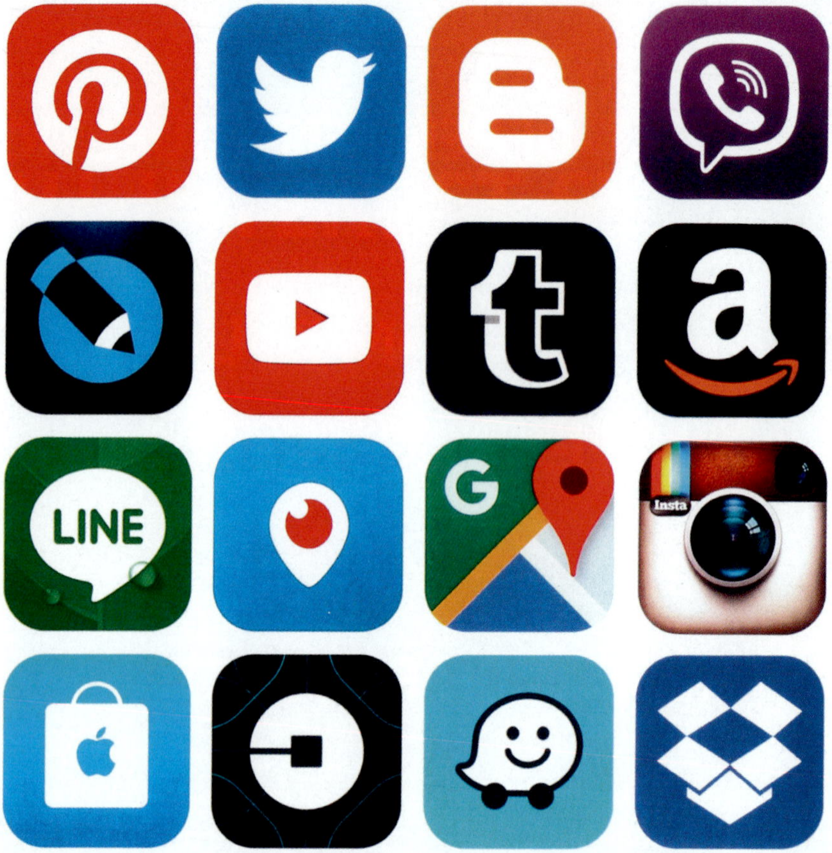

WORDS TO UNDERSTAND

logo—an identifying symbol

mosaics—surface decorations created by small, colored material such as glass or ceramics to form pictures or patterns

target audience—a specific group of people toward whom a marketing campaign is directed

CHAPTER 4

ART IN SOCIAL MEDIA

Social media and art intersect in many different ways. Social media site design, logos, and graphic design created to help marketers attract new customers are a few examples of the way that art makes a difference to the users of all social media platforms. Social media is also changing the way that the world sees and distributes art, and it is also a major source of inspiration for many artists to create statement pieces that teach us something new about ourselves and the world that we live in.

SOCIAL MEDIA SITE DESIGN

You have probably seen the colors and graphics on social media more than a few times, but have you ever stopped to think about who curates these things when building the website? The layout of any social media page, be it Instagram, Facebook, Twitter, or Snapchat, is itself art. These pages are designed to be visually stunning, enticing, and engaging for users like you.

Page Layouts

The way a social media page is curated is a testament to art. Both the mobile and desktop versions of these platforms are designed to be simple enough to avoid overwhelming users while remaining aesthetically pleasing enough to entice them to continue using the app or website. Website designers create the flow of Facebook, Instagram, and Twitter feeds to appeal to the masses when it comes to how a web page looks. This means that designs are made to look great to people from all different ages and walks of life, which is a big job for any artist!

Featured Photos, Cover Photos, and Albums

When scrolling through your own profile, you have probably seen several artistic aspects of social media, but you might not have taken notice of them before. For this example, consider Facebook. Three artistic components of any Facebook page include featured photos, cover photos, and albums.

Facebook's featured photos consist of nine digital frames that users can customize with their own photos. These frames are square and constructed to look like what the art world calls a collage. Each photo takes up the same amount of space, and there is a border around each one. When all the spots are filled, a larger square is completed, which is appealing to the eye.

Another artistic component of a Facebook page is the cover photo. This appears at the head of the page and is designed for a portrait-oriented image. Some people choose to insert photos of things here that are important to them, such as children or pets.

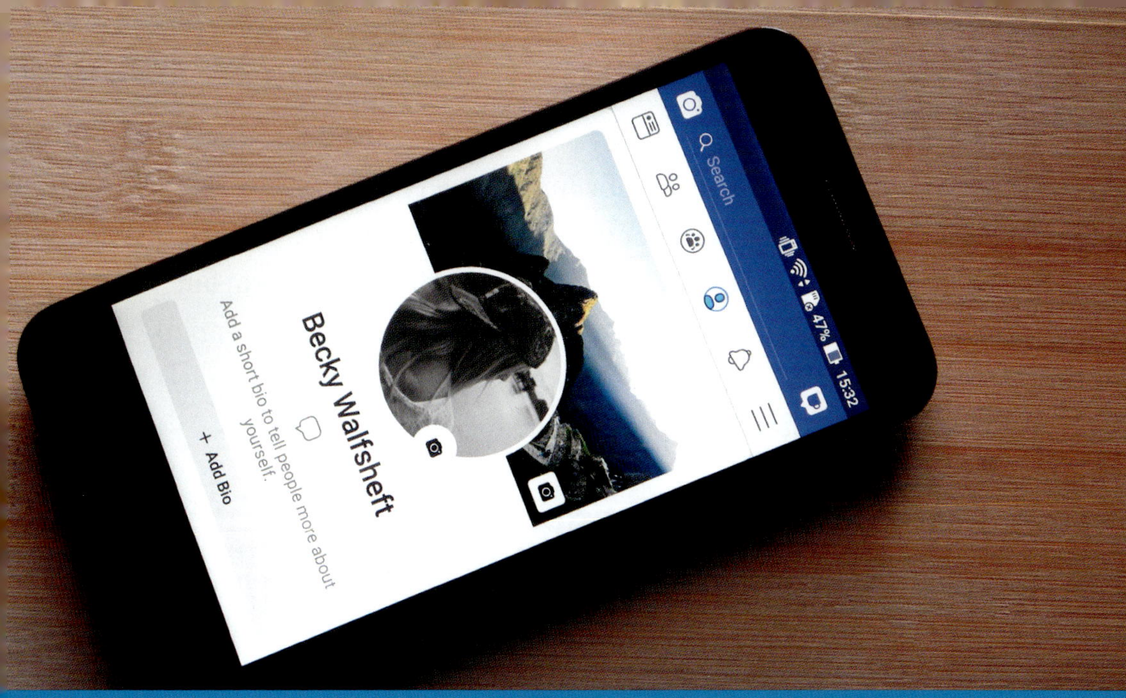

A user's Facebook profile page includes the opportunity for artistic expression through the cover photo.

Others might insert an image that they find striking. Either way, this portion of a Facebook profile acts as a canvas that people utilize to display what they consider beautiful.

Photo albums offer a wonderful way for people to showcase images they want to share. Since photography holds an important place in the art world, these photo albums certainly count as art when it comes to social media. It doesn't matter whether the Facebook member is a professional photographer or simply captures moments on a mobile device that mean something to him or her. The end result is a gallery of emotions and visual depictions of what this person's life might look like—it is an artistic expression.

SOCIAL MEDIA LOGOS

Logo design is an art in its own rite. The small logos that represent social media platforms might not seem to be a way of artistic expression, but that couldn't be further than the truth. Logo designers are responsible for creating a simple, eye-catching design that not only represents the brand or social media platform but also tells the story of the brand for all onlookers. The Twitter bird, Snapchat's ghost, Facebook's f and Instagram's camera are all pieces of art instantly recognizable to millions.

The History of Logos

The history of logo design traces all the way back to ancient Rome. All around the city, people could find **mosaics** that told the story of ancient tradesmen. A mosaic of an elephant would indicate travels

Mosaics are one of the world's oldest art forms.

to Africa. A picture of a dolphin would indicate that a tradesman was a fisherman or otherwise dealt with fish. All these images were telling of the people that they represented, and they are the earliest forms of logos that historians have studied to date.

As technology advanced and e-commerce became more and more popular, the way that people thought about logos changed. Companies wanted a way to represent their personalities and a way to brand their business so that people would know which products originated from which companies. These ideas birthed the first commercial logos.

Logo Design

When an artist sits down to create a logo, there are several things that he or she needs to consider.

First, a logo needs to be memorable. This means that the color scheme must be pleasing to the eye, and the curves and shapes have to be well-thought-out and purposeful. A great logo also has to

Logos that are effective have a design that is memorable and representative of the brand.

ROCK N' ROLL!

Logo design extends to almost any piece of media that you can imagine. If you have ever looked at the cover of a classic rock music album, you have probably seen a logo. The band AC/DC has a quintessential logo that appears on the front cover of their *High Voltage* and *Let There Be Rock* albums. This logo features a lightning bolt and is their most well-known emblem. This design was created by logo designer Gerard Huerta, who also created album logos for Blue Oyster Cult, Willie Nelson, and Bob Dylan.

be appropriate for the brand it represents, so artists must be aware of the attitude or personality that a brand embodies and then they must incorporate that into their final design. Lastly, logo designers must make their final product versatile enough that it looks the same no matter what scale it is or where it is used. Whether it is being used in a small corner of a website or on a giant billboard, it has to look refined and no matter where it is being displayed, people should know what brand it represents.

Perhaps one of the most important things that artists consider when creating new logos is their longevity. When a company uses a new logo, it takes time for people to start recognizing it and associating it with their brand. Consequently, in addition to all the other requirements, the logo art created must be able to stand the test of time. So, logo artists must be disciplined in their craft because they aren't able to rely on current trends in the arts to inspire their designs. They must pay attention to what is going to look fresh and new both now and 10 years in the future.

SOCIAL MEDIA GRAPHIC DESIGN

All the graphics that we see on posts on social media platforms like Instagram and Facebook are the work of artists. These images might initially be created with pen and paper, or in some cases, using digital means such as tablets or computers. Even though they are often created to serve a purpose, like selling a product or spreading an idea, graphics on social media are there to connect with a **target audience**, which is what art is all about.

Tailoring Graphics for Each Platform

Artists who create graphics for social media can't simply draw up their vision and post the raw file across each site. Since each platform has its own rules for sizing, resolution, and types of

Users need to adapt their images to fit the platform they are using.

graphics, completed images have to be modified to work best with whatever site they are being posted to.

To illustrate this point, consider Facebook versus Instagram as an example. In order to get the best resolution and display on Facebook, a photo should measure 1,200 x 630 pixels. Instagram, on the other hand, has an optimal image size of 1,080 x 1,080 pixels. This means that if a social media graphic designer were to post an image on Facebook first and then take the same image to Instagram, major design elements could be cut out of the image.

Graphic Design and Social Media Marketing

When it comes to social media marketing, graphic design is a must. In 2017, a survey showed that 90 percent of businesses were using social media to market themselves or their product. In a marketplace often crowded with options for consumers to choose from, graphics are imperative if marketers want to stand out.

In other words, creating striking visual imagery could impact the profitability of a campaign solely based on how many social media users interact with its posts, so it's very important that consumers are enticed to stop scrolling and pay attention to the product that's being presented to them.

There are many ways that social media marketers use art to help their pages stand out. Small boutiques and shops use models to display their clothing and accessories in a way that makes people want to wear their products. People who market classes and certifications are trying to sell a dream, so they might share imagery that depicts happiness, freedom, and financial success.

Graphic design artists aim for designs that will stand out in a crowded social media marketplace.

SOCIAL MEDIA FRIENDLY ART EXHIBITIONS

Social media has opened the door for artists to create immersive art exhibitions that appeal to fanatics of Instagram, Facebook, Twitter, and Snapchat. These exhibitions feature installations and backgrounds that are perfect for selfie culture, allowing people to take striking images and share them with their friends online.

One such type of exhibition, curated by Japanese contemporary artist Yayoi Kusama, features paintings, sculptures, and "Infinity Mirror Rooms" that are well-loved by Instagram users from all over the globe. There are 10 permanent versions of these around the world. This exhibition is so popular that when it opened in Los Angeles, 50,000 tickets sold out within the first hour. Each ticket included a

This video shows what Yayoi Kusama's "Infinity Mirror Rooms" look like.

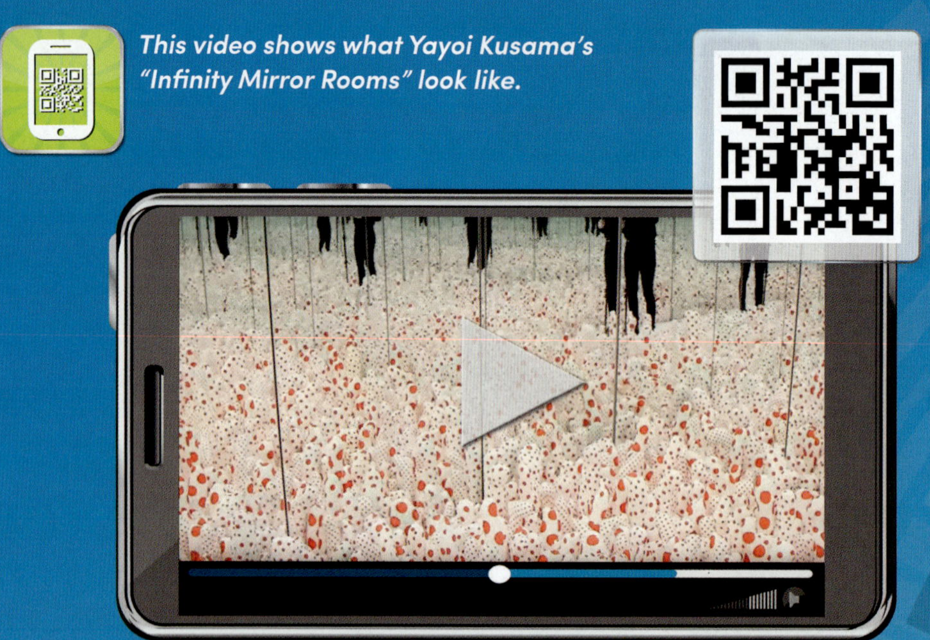

30-second entry to the Infinity Mirror Room, which is teeming with glimmering lights, suspended glowing objects, and a kaleidoscopic effect that is a must-have selfie opportunity.

VIRTUAL ART GALLERIES

Instagram has enabled artists to display their galleries without ever leaving their couches. By simply uploading an image of their work, they can instantly share their latest work with their fans and followers. Consequently, art can sell in an instant and make an impact on the world in a matter of minutes. Gone are the days where art enthusiasts had to wait in line for hours to see an exciting new piece—all they must do now is log on to their platform of choice and start scrolling.

With Instagram, artists can choose to share any of their creations with followers at any time.

This has created a new space for art collaboration, sharing, and even criticism. Nowadays, artists can talk about their vision, create new art, and inspire one another by sending a quick message or sharing a raw file. In an age where instant gratification has become king, the art industry is finally able to keep up with the demand of the masses. Additionally, since artists no longer have to travel the globe to create a piece of art together, pieces that may have never had the chance to exist now grace our Instagram feeds with their presence.

Another important aspect that social media has brought to the art industry is criticism. Social media has created a platform in which art critics have diversified and multiplied. This means that more critics from different backgrounds and walks of life are present than ever before, especially since they don't have to visit an art museum to get a feel for the artwork. Additionally, the feedback is instant and easy to access, since social media provides an easily accessible, diverse platform for critics to do their work.

TEXT-DEPENDENT QUESTIONS

1. What is one thing that an artist must consider when creating a new logo for a client?
2. What is a collage?
3. Which artist is famous for her "Infinity Mirror Rooms"?

RESEARCH PROJECT

Logos are essential to the recognition and professionalism of many businesses and brands today. Choose a social media logo and research the story behind its adoption. Then, create a presentation that includes a short biography on the creator(s) of the logo, and the inspiration behind it. Consider the following questions in your report:

1. Why do you think the logo you have chosen has become so easily recognizable?
2. In your opinion, what makes the logo you chose timeless?
3. Is there anything that you would add to the logo that would make it more eye-catching or that you feel might tell a better story of the brand? If so, what would you add and why?
4. Are there any emotions that this logo makes you feel? If so, what are they, and why do you think you feel them?

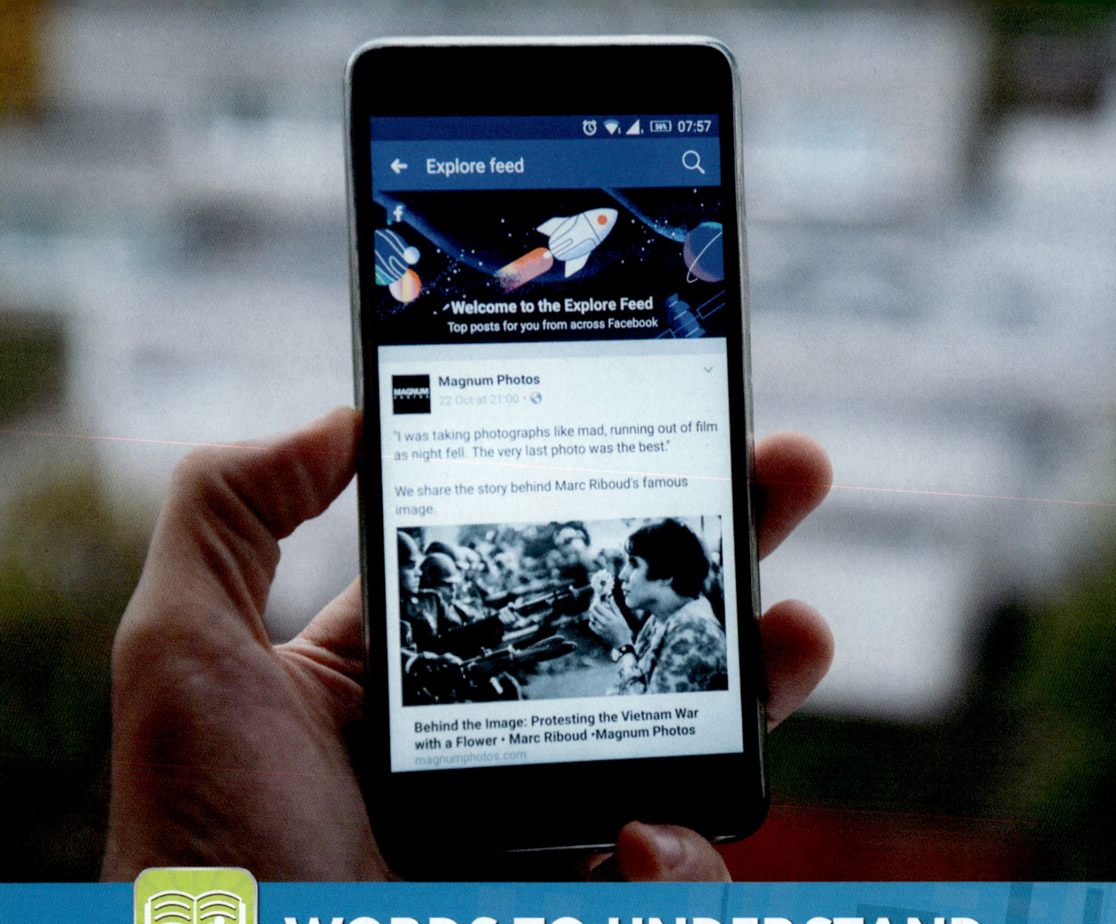

WORDS TO UNDERSTAND

chronological order—the sequence of events that are organized according to when the events occurred, typically from earliest to latest

equations—a combination of mathematical processes designed to find a specific solution

spam posts—annoying or malicious posts on social media or elsewhere on the internet that serves little to no purpose to users

CHAPTER 5

MATH IN SOCIAL MEDIA

Social media and math might not seem to have a discernable connection, but when you look beneath the surface, there are several ways that math helps enhance users' experiences on social media. In social media platforms, mathematical algorithms are used to determine which posts users see, based on their interests and the types of posts they usually interact with.

ALGORITHMS AND SOCIAL MEDIA

Perhaps one of the most prevalent math concepts regarding social media is that of algorithms. Every social media platform out there uses them, and they serve a great purpose to users on each platform. Not only do these algorithms help us see posts that are relevant to our needs and interests, but they also filter out **spam posts** and content that we don't want to engage with, and even help us locate the best results when we complete a search for something.

Several complex algorithms are involved in allowing users to share, post, comment and like at the touch of a finger.

The inputs used to build these algorithms that operate on social media networks today were generated by a collaboration of highly trained software engineers, content strategists, data scientists, and an even more extensive team of people. These teams work together to ensure that everything we see on their social media platform serves a purpose to their users. This makes the social platforms that we use work for us since algorithms allow them to be personalized to our specific tastes and interests.

Post Filtering

Although each social media network uses its own **equations**, the "jobs" that their algorithms do are similar. The first job of many of these algorithms is to filter posts based on relevancy to the user rather than the time of day a post was created. Some factors that might go into determining how relevant a post is includes how many comments are on the posts, how many people "like" or "share" it, and who created the original post. For example, a post shared by a trusted news website might show up on your feed before one from a smaller, less well-known source will.

The algorithm that determines which posts appear in a user's feed uses a unique combination of math equations to calculate the value of every post on the platform. For example, the number of comments might carry more weight than the number of likes, since multiple comments indicate that the post in question sparks conversation. After all, social media is meant for just that—social interaction. Using these algorithms, sites like Facebook and Twitter can narrow down the noise on our social feeds, making the experience more enjoyable and engaging as a result.

These statements are true for sites like Facebook and Twitter, but Instagram's algorithm works differently. When the site first launched in March 2016, its algorithms worked very similarly to its counterparts'. However, in response to a higher demand for fresh, new content, Instagram changed their post filtering to show postings based on when photos were uploaded in **chronological order** from newest to oldest.

Prioritizing Relevant Posts

Another way that algorithms help to enhance what we see on social media is by determining what types of posts we are interested in. These algorithms work by collecting data regarding how we interact with certain posts online. This means that any time we engage in conversation on a post, the platform will store that information and factor it into the algorithm. Therefore, the more we interact, the better the algorithm knows us.

This cache of information is inserted into an equation that figures out what percentage of posts relate to a certain subject matter. Posts that are similar to things that we have liked or engaged with in the past are then moved to the top of our feeds. Posts that we are less likely to engage in are either moved down on the roster or not included in our feeds.

This quick video gives a brief overview of how the Facebook algorithm works to help us see more of what we value on social media.

In modern society, social media algorithms might know us better than we know each other.

Even though Instagram organizes its feed in such a way that the newest posts show up first, relevancy is not entirely disregarded. Its algorithms are also geared toward showing you posts from pages that you have been a fan of in the past. In other words, if you interact with a particular person more frequently than others, their posts will show up ahead of content from sources that you don't interact with, and in order from newest to oldest.

Enhancing Search Queries

Algorithms are also responsible for helping us complete searches on social media. Any time someone searches for something on social media, such as a page, a person, or a product, that information is banked into a database. Then, math is used to determine what is most commonly searched for on the platform.

The search function on Instagram is one of several functions driven by algorithms.

MAKING ALGORITHMS WORK FOR BUSINESS

The online content-creation industry is geared heavily toward understanding how algorithms work and writing content that helps push posts to the top of the user's news feeds. This process, called Search Engine Optimization, works to maximize traffic by helping algorithms understand what type of content a post offers.

If you have ever begun typing something into the search bar on Facebook and the rest of your thought auto-populates, you can thank algorithms! This mathematical equation makes our lives easier by standardizing searches, meaning that our results can be better curated and, therefore, more useful to users.

Instagram's search feed is organized a bit differently, but algorithms still help determine what you see when completing a search on that platform as well. One unique feature that Instagram offers is a "Discover" page. This page includes posts, accounts, and videos that are similar to other things that you express interest in on the platform. This information is collected similarly to how data is collected on other social media platforms.

ALGORITHMS AND SNAPCHAT

One of the most popular features that Snapchat offers is its interactive filters that allow users to insert images over their faces in real-time. The algorithm that is responsible for the facial recognition that makes these filters a possibility is called the Viola-Jones algorithm.

This algorithm, which was first created in 2001 by Paul Viola and Michael Jones, detects facial features in two steps: training and detection. Training involves the process of feeding information into the algorithm that allows it to detect faces with accuracy and precision. Detection does exactly what it sounds like: detects features.

When creating the algorithm, Viola and Jones fed it 4,960 manually labeled images of people of all different shapes and sizes, and who had radically different facial features. In order for the algorithm to work at full capacity, though, it must also know what is not a facial feature. To facilitate this information, the pair inserted 9,544 non-facial images for comparison. The algorithm then uses preset mathematical equations to identify which are faces and which are not. As more and more people insert their images on social media, the algorithm becomes more and more "smart," resulting in more accurate facial detection overall.

There are a few steps that the algorithm takes to detect faces within Snapchat. First, the software converts the colors in the image to grayscale, since it is easier to detect facial features that way. Then, the image is split up into grids. The algorithm then uses a box to highlight each grid until the face is located. The types of features that the algorithm looks for are closely related to math.

The Viola-Jones algorithm looks for what is called Haar-like features. Named after Hungarian mathematician Alfréd Haar, these features are broken up into three categories: edge features, line features, and four-sided features. Each of these features helps the program to understand and detect the outline of the face as well as the features such as the nose, eyes, cheeks, and forehead.

The math within this algorithm is used to help determine where to search for specific features on the face. For example, an equation is used to calculate how far apart average eyebrows are or to establish the average length of a nose. These calculations are useful, especially when filters that place a flower crown on the subject's head or sunglasses over their eyes are used.

The Viola-Jones algorithm was designed to detect faces from the front, so if you were to use Snapchat, you would find that the recognition software works much better when taking a photo from the front rather from the side of your face. In fact, without a full-frontal image of your face, the recognition software often won't work at all. For this reason, it is important to remember that while algorithms are versatile and designed to work with great accuracy, parts of the equation, such as the orientation of the face, must be in order so that they can operate correctly.

Hungarian mathematician Alfréd Haar developed the series of square shaped functions used in modern facial recognition in 1909.

SNAP THAT

Snapchat's quirky and fun facial filters are part of the reason why the platform is so popular among people all over the world today. Team Snapchat estimates that somewhere between seven and nine million people joined the platform in 2019 solely to use the filtering software that the app is famous for.

USING SOCIAL MEDIA IN MATH CLASS

Even though social media is a way for us to connect with friends and family members, read and gather information, shop and interact with companies, and more, that's not all it's good for. Many teachers today also use social media to demonstrate mathematical processes that might otherwise be difficult to solicit interest in. This is particularly true for the subject of graphing in math class.

Social media is largely a network of different people, all interacting with one another. In math, each person would be defined as a node or a point on a graph. When we interact with another person on social media, a line of communication is opened, which would be illustrated as a line on a graph. Using these social media examples to explain graphing, students can gain a deeper understanding of its concepts, and they might have a little fun along the way too.

Another way that social media is being utilized in today's classrooms is to encourage interaction, debate, and engagement

Social media is being used to encourage engagement in college classes.

in college classrooms and beyond. By integrating the tools that social media offers such as the ability to debate in the comments section, the opportunity to candidly react to certain information, and the capability of starting "groups" for people who share like-minded interests, some college classrooms have been able to solicit a higher level of class engagement and more.

Additionally, since social media and the devices through which it is accessed are known to cause distractions in class, harnessing the capabilities of these platforms transforms the distraction into productivity and has also been shown to solicit more interest from students while learning a new subject or studying something as ordinary as math. This could mean that test scores and grade point averages are positively affected, since engagement and interest in school have been shown to positively impact results.

TEXT-DEPENDENT QUESTIONS

1. Who created the algorithm responsible for facial detection in Snapchat?
2. How does Instagram's algorithm organize images on its platform?
3. What is a spam post?

RESEARCH PROJECT

Math plays an important and considerable role in the world of social media. Without it, the information and posts that we see online would be less personal, which might impact the role that it has on our engagement overall—this in turn could be bad news for the social media marketing sector. First, research how seeing relevant content affects the way we spend our money online. Then, explain what you think might happen if algorithms didn't filter the advertisements we see according to our interests. Consider the impact that this would have on both the consumer and the supplier of products and services. Finally, write a one-page report detailing your research, findings, and opinions.

FURTHER READING

Carrigan, Mark. *Social Media for Academics*. London: Sage Publications, 2019.

Roughgarden, Tim. *Algorithms Illuminated. Part 1: The Basics*. San Francisco: Soundlikeyourself Publishing, 2017.

Victionary. *Insta-Perfect: Creative Photography for Social Media*. North Point: Victionary, 2019.

White, Alex W. *The Elements of LOGO Design.* New York: Allworth, 2017.

INTERNET RESOURCES

http://info.cern.ch/hypertext/WWW/TheProject.html
This link leads to a visual representation of what the world's first web page looked like.

https://blogs.plos.org/blog/2019/05/23/hashtag-scicomm-how-social-media-platforms-are-shaping-the-future-of-science
This website explores the different ways that social media might impact the future of science.

https://uxplanet.org/many-faces-of-graphic-design-what-graphic-designers-do-b73a0e611115?gi=3ad80c8de8f0
This website is dedicated to discussing the different roles that graphic design plays in the world.

https://www.engineering.com
Engineering.com is a website whose mission is to help engineers become better in their field. This website offers plenty of information about how to use engineering to create or optimize certain web pages.

https://hiring.monster.com/employer-resources/job-description-templates/software-engineer-job-description-sample
A resource reviewing the job duties of a software engineer.

EDUCATIONAL VIDEO LINKS

Chapter 1: http://x-qr.net/1LRw

Chapter 2: http://x-qr.net/1L6k

Chapter 3: http://x-qr.net/1KxD

Chapter 4: http://x-qr.net/1Jjs

Chapter 5: http://x-qr.net/1LZT

INDEX

AUTHOR BIOGRAPHY

Mary Elizabeth Dean is a teacher and author who is passionate about writing books that not only educate but also inspire. A teen mom and high school drop-out-turned grad-school success story, her ultimate desire is to encourage other "underdogs" to find their own unique path and life's purpose. As a Louisiana transplant by way of Tennessee, Mary enjoys trips to New Orleans, reading forgotten classics, and hunting for treasures in thrift stores with her children.

PHOTO CREDITS

Shutterstock.com
Pg. 1, 32: Syda Productions, 6: ra2 studio, 9, 46: Rawpixel.com, 11: Peter Snaterse, 13: Sylvia sooyoN, 15: Daniel Krason, 16: 1000 Words, 17: JaysonPhotography, 19: Bogdan Sonjachnyj, 20: AlesiaKan, 22: silverkblackstock, 24: Yanawut Suntornkij, 26: Eloku, 28: Kseniia Perminova, 29: Corepics VOF, 34: Kaspars Grinvalds, 36: Twin Design, 39: Faizal Ramli, 41: AN Photographer2463, 43: PixieMe, 45: Gorodenkoff, 48: wk1003mike, 50: SvetaVector, 54: ChameleonsEye, 55: Tortuga, 57: tulpahn, 59: REDPIXEL PL, 61: nito, 62, 76: Lenka Horavova, 64: Pe3k, 66: chainarong06, 68: fizkes, 74: ESB Professional

Wikimedia Commons
Pg. 72: author unknown

Dreamstime
Pg. 53: Maneesh Upadhyay, 69: Burak Tu╠êmler